Client Log

This log belongs to

Clients Name	Appointment Date	Appointment Time	Paid / Owed

Notes

Clients Name	Appointment Date	Appointment Time	Paid/Owed

Notes

Clients Name	Appointment Date	Appointment Time	Paid / Owed

Notes

Clients Name	Appointment Date	Appointment Time	Paid/Owed

Notes

Clients Name	Appointment Date	Appointment Time	Paid/Owed

Notes

Clients Name	Appointment Date	Appointment Time	Paid / Owed

Notes

Clients Name	Appointment Date	Appointment Time	Paid/Owed

Notes

Clients Name	Appointment Date	Appointment Time	Paid/Owed

Notes

Clients Name	Appointment Date	Appointment Time	Paid / Owed

Notes

Clients Name	Appointment Date	Appointment Time	Paid/Owed

Notes

Clients Name	Appointment Date	Appointment Time	Paid/Owed

Notes

Clients Name	Appointment Date	Appointment Time	Paid/Owed

Notes

Clients Name	Appointment Date	Appointment Time	Paid/Owed

Notes

Clients Name	Appointment Date	Appointment Time	Paid/Owed

Notes

Clients Name	Appointment Date	Appointment Time	Paid/Owed

Notes

Clients Name	Appointment Date	Appointment Time	Paid / Owed

Notes

Clients Name	Appointment Date	Appointment Time	Paid/Owed

Notes

Clients Name	Appointment Date	Appointment Time	Paid/Owed

Notes

Clients Name	Appointment Date	Appointment Time	Paid/Owed

Notes

Clients Name	Appointment Date	Appointment Time	Paid/Owed

Notes

Clients Name	Appointment Date	Appointment Time	Paid/Owed

Notes

Clients Name	Appointment Date	Appointment Time	Paid/Owed

Notes

Clients Name	Appointment Date	Appointment Time	Paid/Owed

Notes

Clients Name	Appointment Date	Appointment Time	Paid/Owed

Notes

Clients Name	Appointment Date	Appointment Time	Paid/Owed

Notes

Clients Name	Appointment Date	Appointment Time	Paid/Owed

Notes

Clients Name	Appointment Date	Appointment Time	Paid / Owed

Notes

Clients Name	Appointment Date	Appointment Time	Paid / Owed

Notes

Clients Name	Appointment Date	Appointment Time	Paid/Owed

Notes

Clients Name	Appointment Date	Appointment Time	Paid/Owed

Notes

Clients Name	Appointment Date	Appointment Time	Paid/Owed

Notes

Clients Name	Appointment Date	Appointment Time	Paid / Owed

Notes

Clients Name	Appointment Date	Appointment Time	Paid/Owed

Notes

Clients Name	Appointment Date	Appointment Time	Paid/Owed

Notes

Clients Name	Appointment Date	Appointment Time	Paid/Owed

Notes

Clients Name	Appointment Date	Appointment Time	Paid/Owed

Notes

Clients Name	Appointment Date	Appointment Time	Paid/Owed

Notes

Clients Name	Appointment Date	Appointment Time	Paid/Owed

Notes

Clients Name	Appointment Date	Appointment Time	Paid/Owed

Notes

Clients Name	Appointment Date	Appointment Time	Paid/Owed

Notes

Clients Name	Appointment Date	Appointment Time	Paid / Owed

Notes

Clients Name	Appointment Date	Appointment Time	Paid/Owed

Notes

Clients Name	Appointment Date	Appointment Time	Paid/Owed

Notes

Clients Name	Appointment Date	Appointment Time	Paid / Owed

Notes

Clients Name	Appointment Date	Appointment Time	Paid/Owed

Notes

Clients Name	Appointment Date	Appointment Time	Paid/Owed

Notes

Clients Name	Appointment Date	Appointment Time	Paid/Owed

Notes

Clients Name	Appointment Date	Appointment Time	Paid / Owed

Notes

Clients Name	Appointment Date	Appointment Time	Paid/Owed

Notes

Clients Name	Appointment Date	Appointment Time	Paid/Owed

Notes

Clients Name	Appointment Date	Appointment Time	Paid / Owed

Notes

Clients Name	Appointment Date	Appointment Time	Paid/Owed

Notes

Clients Name	Appointment Date	Appointment Time	Paid/Owed

Notes

Clients Name	Appointment Date	Appointment Time	Paid / Owed

Notes

Clients Name	Appointment Date	Appointment Time	Paid/Owed

Notes

Clients Name	Appointment Date	Appointment Time	Paid/Owed

Notes

Clients Name	Appointment Date	Appointment Time	Paid/Owed

Notes

Clients Name	Appointment Date	Appointment Time	Paid/Owed

Notes

Clients Name	Appointment Date	Appointment Time	Paid/Owed

Notes

Clients Name	Appointment Date	Appointment Time	Paid/Owed

www.ingramcontent.com/pod-product-compliance
Lightning Source LLC
Chambersburg PA
CBHW072213170526
45158CB00002BA/581
* 9 7 8 1 0 9 9 1 3 9 0 2 4 *